W9-AVH-495

book of
grass

JV Brummels

Book of Grass
by JV Brummels

Copyright © 2007
ISBN: 978-0-9769935-3-7
$16.00

Except for brief quotations in reviews, no part of this work may be reproduced or transmitted in any form or by any means, electronic or mechanical, including photocopying and recording, or by any information storage or retrieval system without the prior written permission of the copyright owner unless such copying is expressly permitted by federal copyright law.

Grizzly Media
85447 Highway 15
Wayne, Nebraska 68787

Cover photograph: "Peromyscus Abounding,"
by Melody Saltzgiver

Author photograph: Lin Brummels
Cover and interior illustration: Catherine Meier
Page-number illustration: Bonnie Mercer

Cover design and layout: Edmund Elfers

Many thanks to the editors of these journals, magazines and anthologies in which many of these poems, some in different versions, first appeared: *The Iowa Review, Matrix, Puerto del Sol, The Chariton Review, Rural Voices: Literature from Rural Nebraska, The Laurel Review, Elkhorn Review, The Midwest Quarterly, Kansas Quarterly, Bison Poems: Of Bison and The Great Plains, South Dakota Review, Talking River Review* and *Concho River Review.*

A performance of "Slant of Light," recorded live January 2004 at the 20th Annual National Cowboy Gathering in Elko, Nevada, is included on the CD *Elko! A Cowboy's Gathering.* Western Jubilee Recording Co.

"Jefe" first appeared in a chapbook by the same name, Torque Publishing, copyright © 2005.

"Bedtime Story" reprinted from *Prairie Schooner* by permission of the University of Nebraska Press. Copyright © 2004 University of Nebraska Press.

"Weather in the Bones" reprinted from *Prairie Schooner* by permission of the University of Nebraska Press. Copyright © 1986 University of Nebraska Press.

Many thanks, too, to Grizz McIntosh, Neil Harrison, Maureen Kingston, Tegan Clark and the members of a number of graduate writing workshops at Wayne State College who critiqued drafts of many of these poems and made them better than I could have alone.

And once again many thanks to Eddie Elfers, without whom this collection would never have appeared in print.

Foreword

These new poems reveal Jim Brummels at his best, and that is damned good indeed. They are at times bawdy, at times humorous, at times philosophical, but always refreshingly well-sustained. Time and again they suggest that the poet understands and accepts that animal and human existence often parallel each other, each adjusting, adapting, doing whatever must be done to sustain its life.

I'd say that at heart Brummels is a rancher, and he is; but at heart he is also a gypsy who cannot resist the urge to go beyond that place he has sunk his roots so deeply into – "to find where / in the journey / the adventure is." And I'd add that he is a clear-eyed realist, and a teacher, one who lives not only in the classroom and on the land, but who is likewise of them. Alongside his students he is a learner, and the boots he wears more often than not have manure on them.

His language derives from both the muck and the sweet clover he walks through. Mare heat. Milk-mild. Pigeyes. Wracked cowlot fences. When the drought finally breaks, he stands outside tasting the rain: "My tongue swelled with it, / and my lips moved as if to nurse." And finally, at heart, Brummels is all heart, which means that in this "dense history of evolution" he does not neglect or forget those friends who suddenly disappear into the timeless maw of death. "I stand in weather atop my world. / The moon showers me with generous light. / In the distance the city my friend left behind / sends its industrial glare into the sky." The friend is quietly and eloquently remembered. He is one of many stories of grass, one who has sprouted and grown and turned from green to brown and, when the time seemed right, reappeared, thanks to a poet who cares enough to make the miracle happen.

William Kloefkorn

book of
grass

JV Brummels

Grizzly Media

for Bill

Contents

Part V

" . . . a number of fundamental changes took place within the hominid family as they adapted to . . . the more open savannah grasslands rather than the tropical forests. The four key events in the evolution of the hominid family were: living on the ground, the adoption of bipedalism which freed the 'hands' for other tasks, growth in brain size, and the development of culture and its transmission through speech. The first two took place among the early hominids; the remaining two, in particular the last, took much longer."

– Clive Ponting in *World History: A New Perspective*

Part 1

Grass Widow

After a cool dry spring the sun
finds a notch in the ozone
and burns through a lens of humidity.
Every pickup fishtails at every gravel corner.
Every driver knows the days are endless
but this season of getting it all done finite.

We adjust, change to fit the weather
the way over time an open wound
becomes a washed-out trace of scar,
and by the time the dry south wind is high
in the heavy heads of the cottonwoods
and my lip has shed its sunburn scab
I'm maybe ready to tell the story
I've tried to say so many times.
Maybe I've got my lip back.

And maybe all I can do is shuffle
the pieces and hold each shard
up to hot sunlight, hoping
for some vibration of recognition,
some whispered part of the whole truth.

A day this spring:
I drive south across two counties,
the wet-paint splatter of drizzle
on the four-lane enough to idle
the chemical rigs in miles of fields,
earth no longer turned, simply
sterilized for a new crop no one wants.

To a courthouse, monumental
above the fastfood arches
and cars lined up for coffee
and some egg and pigmeat sandwiches,

maybe some flash-fried potatoes.

Past deputies and metal detectors,
the new terrific security,
to stand beside this young mother
at her arraignment. Her men are gone,
the first to a new woman north of the river,
the next to the place junkies go in lieu of jail.

What's behind it all? Some handy
farm or household chemicals
distilled and needled to the blood.
I witness her sign away her children.

The hanging judge harangues.
The silent reporter keeps it all in shorthand.
The marshal clasps his hands behind his back.
This present carries the weight of the past
like a heavy pistol high on the hip.

Back years: In the day
of zero tolerance and just say no,
thank you, I hold this woman
a girl no bigger than a whisper
on my lap while hand joins hand
joins hand as the joint is passed
around the kitchen table.

Back years again: WPA workers
finish pouring the counted tons
of concrete of this courthouse,
paint the halls and offices,
scatter ashtrays and spittoons
around the courtroom
where they'll be handy
for snuffdippers like me.
And again: Just a meeting of two rivers,

some plank shacks on a mud street,
prostitutes waving from spindly balconies,
grass waving from the treeless hills above.

And somewhere anchored on that green sea
a young mother waits at a table in a soddy,
dust sifting on the fine-haired heads
of her toddling children, for a husband
gone after gold or the herds, his distant death
by drowning or bad horse or lightning bolt
bad news the wind is whispering.

The Wild Poem

– "The moral high ground's the cheapest real estate in the world."

A fullblood I met
told me Lakota
has no word for wilderness.
Teachers taught me Puritans –
my forefathers – coupled
wilderness and evil. Some
claim this is the last
holy land. Here,
at ninety-four hundred feet,
the Department
of Interior sign
makes it official
Wilderness.
What else do we know
for sure? Every square foot
of earth's numbered
by global positioning satellites.

I'll select my own
pedigree, and pilgrims have
nothing to do with me,
except I fit my feet
with care between rocks
in tracks of those
who've made this trek before.
What to think, when
long shadows from high rocks
so ancient they may be
all we ever know of eternity
crawl through the thin air
to us? That the wild geography
we long to learn always lies
only just beyond.

Long Shadows

All day my partner and I go around
this new parcel of the heifers' winter range,
dragging brittle barbwire out from under years
of fenceline grass to tack to broken posts,
resting after every stretch, holding our breath
when we turn back to see if the spells
we use to resurrect this ghost will last,
can contain this season the high bench of cornstalks,
the sheltering trees bunched on the morning slope,
the thick rope of cattail-choked willows
thrown slack along the draws that head Sand Creek.

Forty years ago this was *farm*,
a picturebook range of barnyard stock,
a brood of children my partner calls to mind
through the day – how all the neighbor kids
tore up the upstairs during card parties,
how they visited back and forth,
the gravel of the road, the dust of the lane
scuffing their brass-eyed lace-up boots.

How the old man and my partner's great-granddad
teamed up, traded work, neighbored,
set these boundary fences,
clamshelled postholes,
planted fresh-cut posts,
unspooled silver wire over the endgate
as the team leaned into the collars,
jingled bits and creaking leather
a song with the meadowlark's post-top trill,
the thick whistle of the thermal-riding chickenhawk,
the coaxing grunts and cusses of the teamster.

This day is late October '99, a season
we'll recall as clear-skied and milk-mild.

JV Brummels

By late afternoon we've had enough for one day.
We sit on the tailgate of the pickup for a smoke.
The sun settling on the bench at our back
throws shadows of stumblebum buildings,
wracked cowlot fences and haywire machines
far out before us toward tomorrow morning's sun.

Do we know anything that the old ones didn't,
even that every enterprise carries the seed of its dying?
Could they guess that only these few generations
of busted sod would grow cattails this high
in a muck of topsoil washed down from hilltop?
That while the cattails climbed the draws
neighbors and the neighbors' children
would flood to downstream towns and cities?
That the shorthorn cows and Hampshire hogs
and banties, leghorns, turkeys and geese and sheep
would all be carried away as if by great water?

Another day of fence repair lies before us.
Then it's just a matter of finding a cowboy or two
to help drive the heifers over the ridge
that divides this watershed from the next.
A meadowlark vies for our attention.
Our shadows stretch darker and farther
while my partner talks still of the old ones
who built this crib or that shed,
how they walked cattle from place to place
in the days, he says, *before we had horses.*

–for David Tobias

Shutting Out the Lights

– "Sufficient to the day the evil thereof."

With no nine-to-five life to fret me,
  only another winter highballing nearer
worries my tenured soul,
and a day crossing *t*'s and dotting *i*'s
is wasted subtraction from that distance.
The computer's lazy time-killing graphic
beckons like a curling finger,
an invitation to start this note to you.
I find the remote for the muted TV
and VCR that everyone else turns only on.
I hit a switch and a modern kitchen goes on standby.
The microwave's digital display winks at me.

Lights left burning across the ranch won't keep
the wolf of weather from nosing around the door.
In the corrals the horses bury long faces
in alfalfa up to their intelligent eyes.
I stand stupid in the barn door,
my hand on the light switch's busted casing.
Summer's miller lies dead on the floor.
Last month's hard frost snuffed out all bugs
but this one fly buzzing the specked bulb.
Hundreds of pelicans buzzed Yellow Banks last month.
I've yet to hear a crane or see a goose, but they're free
to travel when weather or impulse moves them.

I hear the pulse of the electric fencer,
the hum and gurgle of the ancient fridge.
All this juice abstracted from world and weather,
channeled and dammed to wait
on my brain's half-hearted electricity
to spark across a synapse.
I shut out the light.

JV Brummels

The moon above my head
is the lightbulb of an idea.
I am what America dreamt,
rich and free to turn a key or saddle a horse
and travel where weather or impulse moves me,
bound only to ride the earth
as it cranks down another notch toward solstice.

I can't believe how full of it I am.
The other half of truth grates.
Snow on winter wind will drift stiff as styrofoam.
I'll channel my puny energy to the care
of an equine, bovine and human family.
The precise stacks of hay bales will dwindle.
One by one I shut out the lights
in the rooms of my head,
double-checking the attic
and gazing long into the cellar.

Only that little night light that comes on
when we first glimpse our mortality burns.
I cross the moonlit yard,
my bones jutting within my flesh,
like lightning or a heavy scrawl.
My boots crawl in the cold dirt.
My shadow marches ahead,
moonglow through the skull.

Life's Work

We hear footsteps in the cellar.
A recliner rocks in the attic.
They steal from our books,
whole pages of our life's work missing.
It's a conspiracy among state and church,
the Departments of Defense, Motor Vehicles,
Homeland Security and our family,
where stealing is a bug
communicated through generations.
They switch cars,
trading up to Cadillac and down to Pinto,
following our crosstown bus.
Kurt Vonnegut, Richard Wright, Ralph Ellison
sit jammed together on a seat
pretending to be themselves.
At least we're not alone –
other writers have been crazy.
If we had the money
we'd hire someone to tail us
to see who it is that follows.
Transmitters in our ears
and along our neural pathways
tell a long history of the Navy
and jail and psych wards and crank.
Cameras peeping out of the light fixtures
above our typewriters record our poems.
We pull in at 3 a.m. from a city hours away.
The dogs in the house bark and bark,
so we drive around till sunup.
We want to know if this one man
has kept our life's work complete.

*

We find his thick, rattled manuscript

and show it to him, talk a little,
listen to him say these crazy things
in a voice sane as canned peaches.
We tell him no one will steal
from him, there's no profit.
We examine what he says
is a driver's license
that's just a photo ID
for the glow, he says,
is around his head,
the telltale features that prove
it's not him at all but his cousin,
the B-movie actor, or maybe,
despite the full beard, some girl.
We see him off in the car
he stole from his girlfriend.
We get ready for work.
Already we're thinking how
to write this up, how to make of it
a little entertainment for this audience.
We'll all laugh, and there'll be the profit.
When we leave, as always,
we leave the doors unlocked.

    —for Dan Roberts and all our imaginary friends

Bedtime Story

This story is colored blue.
For two days we watch them come through.
Now and again, palominos and sorrels and bays
in every brown hue of shining summer-hide sell,
but mostly we see blue, blue, blue.

Of all the quarterhorses in the world,
George says, *only one percent are roan,*
and of all the roans in the world
only ten percent are blue.

This story is a dream I replay before sleep –
the dryland corn north of the city of North Platte
already disked under in this year of drought,
the South Platte a sick woman in a wide bed
of sand. Behind the barn all the boys' talk is
a scarcity of grass. No one offers a toke,
not even as a joke. No laughing matter.

We've come from half the states
and provinces of North America,
a conference of snoose-eaters
beneath a circus bigtop –
snapping canvas and taut guylines,
sideshow vendors of silver-mounted bits
and gal-leg spurs sporting three-inch rowels,
rawhide bosals and plaited horsehair,
bright buttersoft chaps and chinks,
everything a working cowboy
collector could conceivably want.

But it's blue theater, too,
the hands outfitted in court colors,
the *patron* of these ninety sections,
these scattered thousands of cattle

and these gathered hundreds of horses
speaks in soliloquy of pedigree,
introduces his family,
his voice breaking at his father,
wheelchair-bound, broken past
where any dude
would put a horse down.

Do we wonder then in Act Two
when this ambitious prince
speaks in an aside to his ringman?
That though we cannot hear the words,
we see that man with such gentle hand
among the colts steel his eye,
set his jaw and blanch?

*

What's behind it all?
Stud horse and mare heat,
cold jaws and knotheads,
pigeyes and yellow teeth,
trail dust and long horn,
bean belly, summer heat
and lightning strike, frostbit ears,
steel shoes and smashed toes,
the lightning kick to the belly,
the shiver beneath the shimmering hide,
the shudder of one going down,
wire-cut horseflesh crawling
with maggots awash in pus,
that floating arc from saddle seeming
eternal before the sudden solid earth.

*

How deep into the cave of dreams dare we crawl?

The long, sick crossing of the Western Sea?
Some Bedouin war, or the Asian steppes?
The full circle of half-horses picking
their way across a bridge of ice?
Turn back to the light
where *la riata* becomes lariat,
where *vaquero* births buckaroo,
where *caballero* evolves to cowboy,
to the busted-up, bent-bone Wyoming waddy
leafing through his scrapbook
to Nebraska in the '40s.
Studying the hammerheads he says,
Horses sure have come a long ways.

Out past the museum display of family buggies,
out here among the back corrals
where George checks on some minor studs,
to this '77 F-Series flatbed
trailering an open blue Texas fifth-wheel
and this border heeler,
his coat and eyes so identically blue
I can't at first see if he's awake
or sleeping amidst the junk under the hitch,
and this young cowboy under his blue feed cap,
the hem of his blue jeans worn to batting
and hooked over his half-inch rowels.

He allows he'd started a couple
for the outfit, but he wasn't *no regular hand,*
you understand, and *yeah, there was some crosses*
some while back that wouldn't *so much buck*
as run away with the cowboys.

George volunteers that these *folks*
sure seem to be *nice people.*

The boy looks away

and shifts from hoof to hoof
like an honest colt caught
by the sloppy reinsman's sneeze,
tongues his butterscotch
candy like a bit,
looks the other way,
opens his mouth to speak,
speaks, and says nothing at all.

Irons in the Fire

He drove an old two-tone Chevy wagon,
so underpowered he named it Moby Dickless,
but then we all ride those older horses,
pick those gentler colts later on.

A branding fire: gray ash and red coals,
blue flame, blackened chunks of wood
and the heads of a dozen irons lying
in the fire, their long shafts going soft.

Each year but this last he stamped calves,
so proud of this work that at Roeder's Fork
he brought a friend, a dude, a sort of
personal photographer to record each brand.

He missed last year down on the river
at Wood Duck, though he was just a town
upstream that day. Just too busy
with some domestic chores, he said,

but I guess he'd seen enough, smelled enough
burning hair, heard enough calves bleating
and cows bellowing, felt enough of that heat.
Funny he didn't see the flashing warning,

feel the rumble bars. A car so dickless
doing sixty when he barreled through the junction.
Certainly, he didn't see the van that broadsided him
before he rode on ahead, dead before the end

of that rolling, pitching, wild ride.

The Names of the Dead

It is the first morning of July,
all sweet high and hot blue,
when the crew removes the signs
that blocked the highway the past year.
I'm tooling home on asphalt
smooth as a barber shave
between naked cutbanks,
grass and wildflower seed
the last task, a bow to be tied
on this gift of new blacktop.
If I pull over on the shoulder
I can climb through air
where hill used to be
and find in swirling dust
knucklebones of limestone,
our only native rock.

But I drive and take stock:
grown children at home, fine and funny;
calves, branded and worked, ride out
the long season towards a distant weaning;
the young horses we've started
learning to go the easy way,
the art of working with heart;
summer pastures awash in grass.
Only my wife's mother,
now traveling the far reaches,
as all life does, roughens
this road and morning.

For years now I give the names
of the dead to the new colts or fillies,
first of the good horses I rode,
later of the cowboys I rode with,
a hoodoo prayer of breath blown through,

a marker more vital than headstone,
a pedigree more persuasive than papers.
Still, each of us is a stranger
riding out of the sunrise
into the town of our life. And
each leaves when she leaves
a ribbon of empty highway
unspooling for eternity.

Part II

Gypsy Road

I'm walking in desert rain
toward downtown casino lights,
new boots wet enough
to conform, wondering
how I got this far –
by car and cab and train,
and by dumb luck

and momentum begun
half a century ago
when first I rolled off
my diapered butt
and humped my way
across kitchen linoleum
to some shining toy
in window light.

This traveling
is my own fault,
a self-assigned lesson
to find where
in the journey
the adventure is –

The taxi's headlights plowing
furrows in flurries of snow,
the wide womb of this backseat,
a last few blocks before
I am delivered
full-term to the depot,
and this cabbie who too
is a writer and poet,

of horror stories and poems
told by aborted fetuses.

The train
with its oddball passengers
too snooty or fearful to fly,
the Chicago stewards
and new wave of hippies,
the German couple
in their brand-new
cowboy outfits.

The cradle sway
on the rails rocks me,
my hand in my pocket,
in my pocket my lucky
silver dollar,
the country I couldn't
watch with eyes fixed
above arc of wheel
shining just past my reach.

Slant of Light

When the day's push of west wind
gasps, then cyclones around,
this big bronc sets to spinning
between north and south and north,
and if my failing sight stretched
from the heights of this perch
I could swing the loop of my eye
a hundred miles to either interstate,
those running slabs, volcanic flow
smoothed and channeled to carry
a heavy world of steel the closest distance
between point and pointless.

And if this bronc and wind don't settle
soon I'll leave this saddle,
this tanned skin of cow stretched
over rawhide, rawhide stretched
and shrunk over a tree
of what all trees are, and land
on earth that gives and gives
but won't give much more than concrete
to the falling timber of this brittle body.

These loess hills hold no rocks
to crack a skull nor scratch a pictograph
to record this or any history,
nor rare earths for trolls to scrabble
out from beneath a grassroot hide,
nor press of the long dead into oil or coal,
and if we melt down here
and are not found we will be
survived only by buttons
and a half-dozen brass conchos.

But if these chaps flap, the wind

turns and the bronc blows even harder,
I might fly away and save my skin
since skin is what I care for,
my own, and the second skin
that I cover with my skin
when I get lucky,
and the grass of earth cattle skin off
each time the earth loops around
the sun the way I'm spinning
from west to east to west
so that in the long light breaking
beneath the skyline clouds
I spin from sundown to sunrise
to sundown, each quick day an aging,
until I grow long in tooth
and the straight line of my spine
curves like a question within a cloud
of fine hoof-raised dust.

Rising day and falling night,
the bronc and I cut and re-cut
the turning light
in our three-dimensional shapes
this way and that and back,
tie hard and fast to the wind
long as we blow. No matter
our other sins, I know
that pounding hoof nor falling man
will leave no worse than they have lived –
light on the land.

The Neighbor Lady

Whichever wag said April's the cruelest month
never spent a gray January on the windy plains,
lowering clouds an angry man's death mask,
earth a smoked-down butt toed out by a dirty boot,
November's snow like phlegm and dry blood,
the sun gone to some state home for the infirm.

This twenty-five-year-old Power Wagon growls
and grinds its load of hay among shell-shocked cows,
the voice in my head telling me to get the hell out
argues with the tinny dash speaker,
WNAX out of Dakota, the Neighbor Lady
punctuating a recipe for dried-beef hot dish

with a dry winter cough. Old people meal, a can
of mushroom soup and cured meat. Without
missing a beat she extemporizes a message
from her sponsor, some cottage-industry
solar-powered Perpetual-Eternal grave flame
suitable for mounting at the foot or on the stone.

I've heard her my whole life – a young war bride
broadcasting a gossipy recipe of helpful hints
to her sisters, Rosie the Riveters returned, doing
their part again, this time in an orgy of population.
Their men in remnants of uniforms smoke
at the table, waiting on livestock market reports.

The war recedes like a new Mercury speeding
down a county road towards town
and Saturday night ballroom dances, television
some rich rumor of a distant jet-powered, pushbutton
future. Some barefoot towheaded kid
sneaks out past his mother, broom in her hands
stock still, an ear cocked to the radio atop

the refrigerator. All he wants to do with the frail jigsaw
he's taken from the pantry is cut another three inches
off the tall cedar stump standing in the chickengrass
of the house yard. If he gets tired, he'll find one
of his many brothers, con him into finishing the job.

He can't know that he'll never do more than scratch
an inch into that cedar, that the thin cut will taunt him
till the day they truck out the stock, pack up the furniture
and TV, and leave. Nor could he see a winter day
so far away as this, so frayed and worn, so grim.
Nor could he hear me, if I had the heart to warn him.

Cantos

I

There's something happening out here, man.
You know something, man?
I know something you don't know.
That's right, jack.
The man is clear in his mind,
    but his soul is mad.
        Oh yeah.
He's dying I think.
He hates all this.
He hates it,
    but the man's ah –
He reads poetry out loud,
    alright?
And a voice, a voice . . .
        –the photojournalist in Apocalypse Now Redux

The boys come and the boys go
but always the same boys
understudies stepping up
out of the woodwork
into a Greek chorus line
happy for the break
eager to say their piece
almost in unison
and then the same initial wonderment
toddling before the concern
discerned in their voices
always at the anticlimax
the same disbelief
the howling condemnation
condescension and consternation.
Constantinople! they curse
like the gods themselves.

II

Two-fitty now, two-fitty when we meet tonight,
and the rest when the job is done.
–Jack McCall in *Wild Bill*

B ut the girls are always The Girl
the slip of sun deep in the cave
casting the shadow
he casts as The Real.
He kisses The Real's cheek
buys her the good Russian vodka
hopes the secrets he tells her
are dirty enough to keep
her sitting at the bar
while he buys another round
and another
and now he knows
he needs The Real because
without The Real
he can't substantiate himself
and he tells The Real that
and he tells everyone in the bar
yelling *I know my heart!*
Why won't anyone listen?
for a second time
and now they turn their heads
back to their drinks
and when he looks
beside him at the bar
he finds The Real –
The Real's gone, man!

III

> *When it comes to women, boys,*
> *I like to keep one in reserve.*
> *It don't take a lot of loving*
> *But it sure takes a lot of nerve.*
> > —Waylon Jennings, *Waymore's Blues (Part II)*

> *Whoop! Whoop! I just made that up.*
> > —Waylon Jennings, *an ad lib*

This man constitutes a footnote
in a test of trivial knowledge
of the arcane if he's lucky.
His favorite movie
and color is blue *Serpico*
though not in that order.
He's got to make some changes.
He's thinking about changing that.
The best advice he ever got
on the subject is
writing is a physical act.
Or was it *activity?*
Anymore he can't remember
anything. He's going to give up
something as soon as he can
put his finger on it
lay hands on it
bless and sacrifice it.
He's going to save his own life.
He's got no choice.
He's a self-made man.
The one-eye kitty winks at him.
The one-eye kitty kind of likes'm.
The one-eye kitty is the one thing
he won't give up
something he wouldn't
change for a dollar
or fitty or a hundred fitties.

IV

> *Fiction . . . seems mainly to be asking*
> *two questions:*
> *Where does the road go?*
> *And how is one to marry?*
>   –Larry McMurtry's *Roads*

It's all in the history books:
The woman was a Real Girl
back in her girlhood
who bared her breasts to the moon
for the cold moonlight's touch
who lay on her back in the dirt
and stretched her arms out and her legs
and caught the moonlight
on her fingernails and her toenails
and swirled her happy hands and feet
hard until the light flew off
in a passing breeze
and became the Milky Way.
But then she had to get up
to do the cooking and the cleaning
and for strength she ate dirt
until she was so full she squatted
and spit out a child. And the child
was the earth and she had to drag
the earth around by the umbilical
while all the time the coyotes yelped
their ghost laughter. And that
is why the moon and earth are shes
and why even old people have navels.
You can look it up.

Bright Lights, Wayne City

County seat and college town
　　shotgunned into an unhappy marriage,
it ain't much, *city* my little joke
on a smug frog in a dry pond,
plenty far from the county's west end
in this old lumber wagon Ford
handling like a hog on ice
and trucking fugly to boot.
I wonder why I'm dressed
in my best black boots and cleanest shirt
when all I want is a comfy chair
to snooze out this winter evening.
Still, with a big wind and snow
and bitter temps tomorrow's certainty,
a cabin-fevered soul has to run
when and where it can,
and once parked on South Main,
my tall heels planted on concrete,
the traffic and snow are loud and dirty
as in real cities I've seen.

Above the streetlamps rides a blessing
of low velvet lavender overcast,
and the southend band's better
than a mopey sinner deserves.
They've got my brand at the bar,
and when friends wave me over
my feet clog-dance to lyrics
no one in a hundred miles knows
but me and the vocalist. I'm free
to sit here without speaking,
and that too constitutes a blessing.
I lean the sound hole of my good ear

to catch voices recounting old stories
and offering happy opinion.

I recall why I've come.
The all of this piddling town is a celebration,
fresh sheepskins tattooed to hearts
at parties at the Legion, the Elks and the Eagles,
in apartments and trailers and houses, in cars
and in beds and on front porches cold as tundra.
I'm here to shut up and listen to each
of the voices up and down this city street –

the wild-haired stutterer's scat,
the speeder's riff
and the hipster's jive,
the stoner's laconic drawl and
      caesura,
the purr of a passing Cadillac
above the bass chord of an unexpected old friend
and the twelve-string giggle of his new friend
expecting their first come spring,
the unborn child's amniotic yodel;
through a club's open door a smoker's laughing hack
and counterpoint squeal of old lady delight;
cymbal crash of big man across the street
calling my name with a smile;
in a parlor deep in this ghetto of blondes
this blonde's guffaw and chuckle
is the thumb swat and finger tickle
across guitar strings, her fine jawline
and the way she holds
her pale drink choreography.

Each heart beats its own rhythm,
each voice box is a reed buzzing to each breathing,
each gesture of hand and lift of eyelid
accompaniment all the way uptown to Logan Street

where my tongue's finally worked loose,
and a loud drunk's late arrival
is a big bass drum over the tinkling triangles
of retirees' polite conversations.
One overstuffed professor's asleep
in his chair, chin on rattling chest,
and even my high-spirited trumpeting
is not enough to wake him, his polite snores
innocent as any infant's, just one ditty
among all the musics ringing in my ears.

—for Scott McIntosh

The Rest of the Story

The crow high in the cedar knows two things:
it's snowing and it's going to snow.
Campus knows only leaden sky and ice
in all its rutted and windblown postures.
Half my friends have cracked their noggins.

*

I've got the Power Wagon half across the curb
in a line of jackknifed and jilted vehicles.
It's the winter the Lutherans warned us of for years,
the one we deserve. I don't have the heart to hear more
Paul Harvey, that trochaic wind-geezer.
I'm reaching for the knob when he says
Elizabeth Ayres. The name's a breeze
seeking lift out of memory's freezer-burnt maze.

*

A simple story: Confronted
by employees of Lord & Taylor,
poet Elizabeth Ayres
claimed security framed her
by planting *in her purse*
an unpurchased brassiere.

*

Well, good day to you too, Paul.
For once, there's news, and thank you.
What poet gets busted for underwear?
With the First Amendment far from secure,
who turns to freeing lingerie
from the chains of capitalist oppressors?

*

And if a matter of principle why dissemble? I suppose
Beth was broke or cheap or crying out for attention
or cracked in the frames of too many winters.

*

The story always is more than we know.
I fly far from this idling truck to a wet fall
far east in our most recent century. I knew
two Beth Ayres, the before and the after,
the rumored details of her breakdown feeding
a workshop legend – *Her roommate left sharp knives
under her pillow. She was playing with her head.*

*

She was our least engaged critic,
her own poems all she spoke well of.
She needed no friends and took no prisoners.
She sneered at our most serious work
and dismissed it like used tissue.
I see all those young faces grow hard.

*

And just when we started to breathe easier,
thinking the hospital or home had her for good,
she – or her good twin – reappeared one sunny afternoon
in a sloppy-wet gush of praise for each poem we presented,
no matter how skilled, honed or finished.
While she bubbled like some kid's sodapop,
we huffed the room blue with cigarettes
and stewed in our bitter juices.

*

When she ravaged a brief, unpretentious verse
with undue superlatives, we shook our chains,
snarled, and attacked that little poem,
snapping at each other to get to it first.
We hamstrung it,
tore out its throat,
drank its small blood,
licked the body cavity clean of organs,
devoured its thin flesh,
shredded its hide with our claws
and picked our teeth with the bigger bones.
Oh, the professor tried to wade in among us,
but the midst of that frenzy was no proper place
for a Maine man in academician's tweeds.

*

Alone, I disposed of the remains of my slight poem,
scratched out a shallow grave in my psyche,
rolled in its essential details and subject,
the particular language it spoke,
even the name by which I called it,
turned and never looked back till now.
A thin thread of radio wave and a needling voice
pull closed the wound of a thousand winter skies.

*

Through the frame of my windshield
gray condenses to green cedar and black crow.
Like all worshippers of story and song,
I already carry the seed
of this windy shirttail relation to that lamb,
some marker for all the poems
abused and abandoned along the way.

*

A story that never ends can't be lost,
and the silver streak in this gray weather
is that long winters make many poems.
The crow caws once
and lifts her shadow out of the cedar, bound
for the edge of some other's circle of sight.

*

I step down out of the truck
onto water solid and slick as a mirror,
place one middle-aged boot
ahead of the other, knowing
that on thick ice
I can go down but not through.

Luck Comes and She Goes

J ays and crows and magpies
   huddle and play and bathe
outside my window by turns
of weather through this winter,
but only today concerns me –

though to pretend in such a bird
as a day orphaned from the flock
of time is a fool's count.

Still, I insist on a single day
like a creationist fitting millennia
of prehistory into a single workweek.

Call it the Ides of March, short and true
as the salt and pepper, a bag of weed
and a blued revolver on a hardwood table.

A day without the fix of coffee,
so contrary to its neighbors
that I drive long as the gas holds out
down highways I've known for decades
stumped for a familiar landmark –

yesterday some ghost,
the surprise visit of that bear
of a horseman, shot-up veteran,
sidearm beneath the tail of his shirt,
to talk the mud and sand of America;
the bald eagle down by Willow Springs –

until I find the Izard cemetery
where pioneers were laid
to rest by a particular sexton
with the bones of Omaha

killed in the big Lakota fight;

the puzzling billboard of Ali
advertising near as I can tell
courage as if we could be
anything but brave;

the roadkill coon laid out
on his back
on the shoulder
of the road
like some pudgy spent lover;

the truckstop's giant American flag
snapping in the late winter wind
to remind me I was born a citizen.

Part III

Jefe

*–"In a world of certain truths a poem might be permitted
one lie."*

The highway runs straight as a taut rope.
Hunters in see-me orange work their dogs
back across fields the size of townships
to new rigs with urban plates parked on the shoulder,
to drive to the nearest town
big enough to support a bar and grill
or a café with a hunters' noon special.

Decades since he hunted, his kid's unbroken fingers
on the stocks of a single-shot Gambles sixteen-gauge.
Chokecherry brush and foxtail-choked stubble.
Before herbicide, pesticide and no-till.
Four families to the section,
the first arithmetic he learned.
When men talked rods of fence,
a formula more vexing than pi.
He liked the walking and liked the gun a lot
but gave it up rather than make sport of killing.

The big Buick is well past the hunters now.
The road cuts across the rise and fall of hills
beneath the clear, blue eye of sky.

Pheasant, a bird adapted
to a new order coming to a new world.
Those farmers of his childhood,
sons and grandsons of immigrants,
younger then than he is now,
still carried the tip of the mother tongue
in church-house hymns
and street-corner egg-and-daughter night confabs,
their town-clothes suit-coats over bib-overalls

under brushed if battered hats.
Any heart is battered,
the generous ones most of all.
His partner has had an attack,
and his mind brims with it
so that he crosses the long bridge
over the Platte without noting either.
Since his wild days this water
and the Big River to the east
have marked the borders of his territory,
his spirit poor and foolish beyond them.

*

Today, he takes his seat
at the head of the table,
and the lawyers and bankers
file in and thank him.
He recalls when first he sat
before a desk in some dusty bank,
hat in hand,
how he mortgaged a piece of his heart,
handed over some parcel of his life,
to that fool across from him.

Today, he throws his hat
in the corner on the carpet.
For two hours they gossip
and miss the point like a bible-study circle
while he washes down snoose with bottled water,
and watches the November afternoon sun
fall through the tall windows,
and remembers when a square room,
a long table and overstuffed chairs
made him hunt the nearest exit.

They conclude their business

and wait on his final word.
Their irritating faces
make up his mind for him.
He tells them a truth
he'd thought to save for a better day,
and they look down and away
while at his left hand
the most sleekly grizzled among them
calls his name and says
His mark.

*   *   *

He's early
and while she dresses
he sits in her one good chair
with the dead phone in his hand
as if he might call someone.
He knows, even in this apartment labyrinth,
the sun's dropping beyond the door at his back,
but the black blinds hide even the echo of sundown.
His heartbeat is lost in the neighbor's music.

He watches this ordinary girl
become more beautiful
each time she steps around the corner
like a nurse checking a patient
whose undiagnosed condition
is the focus of her shift.
While she pokes a fresh earring
through a pink lobe
she asks if he's staying the night.
He tells her what he always tells her,
when he can – what she wants to hear.

He washes his face and hands
and combs his thin hair.

JV Brummels

They meet friends for supper.
He knows what he's here for –
the girl's waterfall of talk,
the flirting, even when it turns mean.
They make up aliases for each other,
inventing other people
to live in their world.

He knows there's no fool like an old fool.
He hears it as a voice from barroom speakers.
She's no fool, just pretty and smart
as a scalpel-cut across a battered finger,
blood oxygenized to true red welling up,
the flesh around the slit already necrotic.

He knows why he's here.
The line of his life stretched
tight as a grass rope
sliced years ago by a faithless wife,
the severed ends still coiling wildly.
What brings him
out under the city lamps
is a young man's faith
in the magic of night
to make it right again.

He knows in the heart he cannot hear
that though this girl loves him
she will not keep him.
He knows that though it can be mended
with stents and sutures
a heart cannot be changed.
He leaves the city in those little hours
when even streets get their rest.

*   *   *

Now he climbs the ladder of rivers
back to his home territory
past fields where tomorrow
hunters will again kill what they love,
a big go-cup of coffee cooling in the console,
past towns abandoned in the dark,
listening to the same music again
and again to remind him what's decided.
Against the speeding screen of concrete,
the high-beams project faces
of partners and friends and neighbors
he's fought for and with and finally against
for some fool's territory he now owns.

*

He runs his ride into the garage,
finds a button in the dark and presses it
to bring the door down behind him.
The last of the coffee is cold
as the best coffee he ever had,
a breakfast pot left on the cold stove
in a half-remembered emergency,
and drunk with the sundown
of a spring thaw day at his back
with a compañero.

Later, they fell out
over winter grazing and water rights,
that man's anger a fire burning
the afternoon air of another November,
while in his mind he measured
the steps to the nearest weapon,
the .30-.30 he keeps to stop the hearts
of critters past getting back up.
To keep the territory of his life
he would put that man past

where this earth's arguments could reach.

Back in the days of subtraction,
when four became three became one,
while abandoned houses and barns fell in
and were dozed in with the rosebushes,
the clotheslines and sandbox toys and outhouses,
burned, and their ashes buried.

Colts he'll pay young cowboys to break
whinny from the corrals.
He walks into a home of photos
of grown and distant children,
empties his pockets,
drops change and folded bills
beside the checks from the day's mail.
His bride sleeps above him.

Coffee.
The story goes
his great-grandma,
a tiny woman,
walked among her neighbors,
mounted Indians,
when they visited,
pouring coffee
and breaking bread.

He takes from the pantry
the special bottle of bourbon
from a long gone birthday,
the last of the glasses he bought
on a trip with his brothers.
He pours it full,
remembers the doctor
wants to see him again.
Looking up

he sees his neighbors,
darkness and age,
standing in the door.

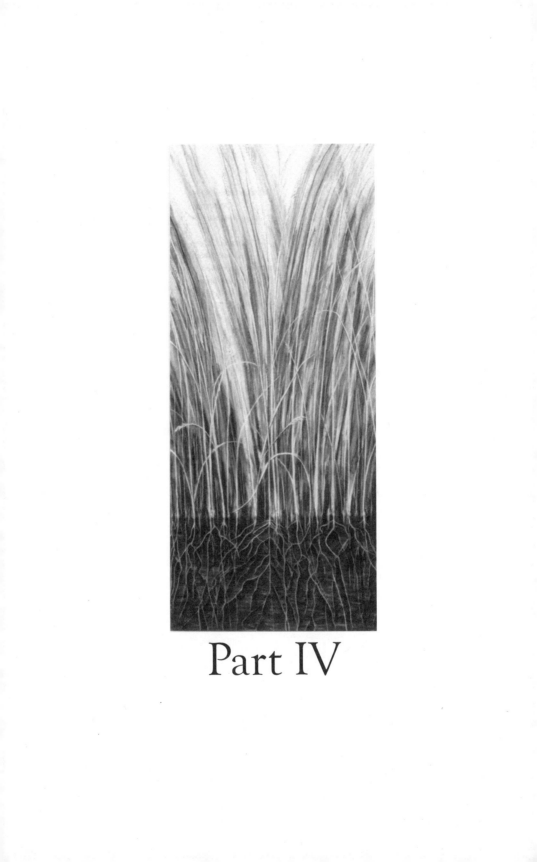

Part IV

Nobody's Business

We moved pairs through a stiff wind
down a few miles of dusty county road.
How many? From where to where?
Ain't nobody's business.

I know a man knows a man
has two children
with a woman not his wife.
His wife knows,
the two kids know.
Hell, even I know,
and now that you do too,
the only one who don't
is the man who's for years
paid child support.

I know a man charged
with abuse for giving
this disturbed kid
his book of poems.
Lost his day job,
got put on the list
of sex offenders
of a major Western state.
If the disturbed can't
take a dose of poetry,
they should give him
some medicine for it.

I know a kid who killed
a man. It was an accident
that could have happened
to me or you or one
of my kids. I know
a man who killed a kid.

JV Brummels

It was an accident, too.

So where those cows left
and where those cows went
and how far they traveled between
ain't nobody's business.

Cowboy Love

– "A poem's worth the paper it's printed on, more or less."

Sunlight-pretty in her yellow sweater,
blonde hair brushed a hundred strokes.
Too often like her father –
her mother likes to say –
too smart for her own good,
but the high winds of her life have twisted
and frayed certainties her mother raised her with,
and risk has yet to cost the price of playing it safe.
She likes thongs and chunky shoes,
has a nipple ring and a tattoo on her hip,
something to pay the bills till she figures
what's next and where it's at.
Twenty-three or -four?
She stops to think.

It's a county seat town on a state highway,
brick streets and a ju-co on the hill,
rigs parked angled to the curb,
an after-hours party on the front porch
of a pair of gay stoners
the first night of spring.
A droopy-lidded heeler stands on two legs
on a tangle of tarp in a pickup box,
tracking who comes and goes.
Fog breathes like white magic
in the haloes of streetlamps.
Naked heads of wet trees
hint of family madness.

She keeps him talking easy as pie,
gets his story in no time flat.
A good hat pushed back on thin hair,
a stiff pair of Levis over tall boots,

he's pushing fifty. He's got a half-ass
sales job keeps him around
town a few days most weeks,
a crooked grin that doesn't show his teeth
and a granddad's glint behind his glasses,
a grazing lease somewhere west and half-interest
in a string of pedigreed horses she'd like to see.

With a sudden friend the bargain we make
is an adventure in talk and time,
travel across language and landscape,
to name what we've thought but have yet to say,
to look together at what we've only seen apart.

They're running a back highway
in a high-mile pickup he long ago named,
when a state pat stops them for a taillight,
looks them over in a flashlight's unblinking beam.
He can't hold but warns them,
cuts them loose with a lecture
on staying within the limit.
The good taillight signals
their way back into traffic
that won't come this way for hours.
Their talk fills the cab.
She smells in his scent some hint.
When she sleeps she speaks
names he cannot know.

She wakes in the milk-light before sunup.
Wind from his open side window
blows her hair before her eyes.
She's farther this way than she's ever been,
a straight highway in a flat grassland
without even the blue twinkle of some security light.

A line of hills is a shadow far to her right.

His eyes half-moons
in the last of the night,
he says, I've been thinking.
I'm not so old,
I'm not your father,
and I'm not that married.

She looks straight ahead to think.
Behind them the sun pops over the skyline
like morning toast,
sending their joined shadow miles ahead
on the vanishing highway.

Paradise, Wyoming

These things happen, a falling backwards
onto this stretch of tangled sheets
across a hard motel mattress,
the mirror across the room coupling a still life
of nightstand and lamp, bottle and plastic cups.

She's learning to drink good whiskey neat,
a habit fit for a woman of experience,
a rattlesnake antidote for a youth she tires of.
Only among the ghosts of thousands of travelers
does the yipping itch within her lie down to sleep.

For now she desires her only children
be those she teaches, whose grandest failures
cannot much mar the triumph of inexorable growth.
For now she will hold this man's hand to her,
blood rising to her skin to meet his fingertips.

Soon enough she will leave this room.
Soon enough will be the last time with this man.
Soon enough the image in the mirror will be
the woman she longs to become.

*

The cowboy, not much inclined to reflection
but troubled in his mind by some passing shadow,
ignores his place in the mirror,
Though his religion is the here and now,
his thoughts jump like dice across a busted past,

to daughters not much younger than this girl,
to better whiskey and the good horses he rode.
He'd hoped to be done forever sorting

the bones of a life already lived.
He'd always only been what he is:

a man with a few good horses
and the knack of a good time.

He wants to ask how these things start,
though he's known, as if forever:
a kind and careful word, the right smile.

His cold snake of a heart pumps thin blood.
He studies the door idly, as if it might open
ever on a better place than this.
He reaches to the floor for his hat.

*

A uniformed boy, a few months on an archaic job,
stands outside the motel-room door,
sweating palm wetting the rubber grips
of the weapon he's used
in Lone Ranger fantasies of saving the day,

protecting schoolchildren and the bank's money,
the sudden and sure coupling of clue and truth
a fevered tangle in his mind.
He can't quiet the heart that hammers
blood to the fingertips of his gunhand,

gorges his eyelids
so that each snake-quick blink tinges red
his vision of the door, the numerals hanging there.
At his back lays an almost empty parking lot.
Beyond, a semi tractor, its jake brakes blubbering,

drags a potload of hereford calves
off the interstate toward an eternity of sagebrush.

JV Brummels

The room lies within his jurisdiction.
The door will open on what's left of his life.

The Rocking Horse

Owner-operator Del Rio's rag runs circles
around a chip in the length of mahogany bar
the UP freighted from Dayton a century ago
before the big blizzards of the eighties
killed the cattle and open-range ranching
and sent the Rocking Horse's builder
packing in the dark of a summer night,
leaving a dozen rim-chipped glasses
and his debts to gather dust.
Del can see him in his mind –
a faceless man on a saddlehorse
trailing mules through the badlands
among the moonlit bones of dead cattle,
the stars strung out behind him
like so many bits of broken bottles,
in his ears the night wind
blowing like a brawl,
night air covering him like a shroud.

Del looks into the dent in the bar,
examines its little diameter
sitting in the left eye of his reflection,
drops the rag on it,
passes his fingertips across his forehead.
He turns to read the cans
of Skoal and Copenhagen,
the half-pints of fruit-flavored vodka
through the glass doors of the backbar,
the redskins in their fishbowl,
the racked sour cream and onion chips,
the dust on the combs and sunglasses
and fishing lures on their cardboard displays,
the flyers of county fairs, rodeos, jackpots
and dances, the estate auction and salebills
strung on a length of baling wire by clothespins

like flophouse sheets on the line.
Business cards of implement dealers and whiskey peddlers
square off beneath a sheet of plexiglass.
A stack of antique beer glasses sparkle
on the bar like an unmounted chandelier.

Del groans at the thought of cash
paid fifteen years ago in Dakota
at last traced to a bank in Utah,
shudders that the whore he married
could give a California parole officer
the postmark of the only letter
he was fool enough to write.
He studies the mural of longhorn
cattle coming up from Texas.

When the bell over the door
makes its little chuckle,
Del's hand goes under the bar.
He nods to two boys.
Through the window the Iowa plate
is confused in the signpainter's cursive.
The backseat is stuffed with camping gear.
Del clicks back the safety
on the twenty-gauge Auto & Teller.
His hand surfaces around a damp rag.

New Day, Central Daylight Time

Again this world turns to the sun.
In marshes the gurgles of purple martins
slide into guttural yawns.
Mockingbirds along roadsides and in thickets
warm up by repeating a phrase a dozen times,
fall silent and wait for a suggestion.
Barn swallows balancing on a wire
take turns sneezing and excusing themselves.
Robins, already up and about,
drop to lawns, one-eye the thatch,
and tut-tut the worms still snuggled in below.
Jays in orchards raise a ruckus,
and in ditches and lowlands,
bouncing on reeds in the breeze,
redwing blackbirds stretch and slur a note.
Meadowlarks on fenceposts trill a crystal whistle
while chickenhawks in haystacks clear their sinuses.
Crows call,
and woodpeckers in dead trees stutter.
Pheasants under cover of sweetclover squawk,
and in stubblefields bobwhites call themselves by name.

In cities along rivers and railroads
and in towns spaced along the highways,
flocks of morning men and women
turn up their faces to check the time,
drain first cups of coffee,
gargle, yawn,
stare into a rain of eyedrops.
Sugar-starved, they open mouths
under the ripped circles of doughnuts,
kick back for a cigarette, cover their eyes
against the light with wire service news,
scan the papers for *This Date In History*.

Outside a twelve-by-twelve steel shed
outside a birddrop town,
a prairie chicken's voice cracks.
Inside, first-day, first-job Neal Scrim,
inside the booth,
mouths his news copy for the thirteenth time,
prays for no late-breaking stories,
leans back in his chair to watch the red
hand sweep the wall clock above him.
He whispers Good morning. It's six a.m.
and KCAN now begins its broadcast day.
He breathes deep, tenses his buttocks
and says Good morning. It's six a.m.
and KCAN now begins its broadcast day.
The red line perches atop the black hand.
He leans forward, keys the mic
and speaks to whatever world listens.

Jackson's Nightmare

The jungle tonight is not the jungle
of Asia but of houseplants
grown larger than a small boy
lost among all the greens
in the big box of Crayolas.
He walks beneath weeping figs and palm fronds
upon a red, white and blue coffee table
in an apartment in San Francisco.
Some weight from outside the dream
says the pistol he carries is real.
Some certainty from his heart
says no one will find him in time.
He runs to a church shrouded in ivy.
Vermiculite sucks at his shoes.
He arrives to find the doors locked.
He turns to a tap on his shoulder
to stare into the fresh wound
of a dead president, to the smell
of blood pumping over a clerical collar.
His screams are drowning
in staccato radio transmission
and the cyclone suck
of helicopters coming in low.

He sits in bed
staring through an open window
tracking the headlights of a pickup
passing on the county road below.
He holds his hand to his slick chest
against the heart that races
until it finds the tempo of the breeze
shifting in the trees outside.
He reaches to the nightstand,
sorts through green government check stubs,

a plastic bag of marijuana.
He finds a pack of menthol cigarettes.
His face is sun and shadow in the Zippo's blaze.
He hefts an overturned ashtray from the floor.
His eyes study the glow
pulse toward him
breath by measured breath.

The Francis Furter Memorial VFW Post, Café and Bowling Lanes

Past the poster-patched and unlatched door,
    past the coffee shop deserted
except for eighty-eight year old Heldegard Hinkmann
standing guard – arms crossed, nose high –
over two dozen deserted cups and saucers,
a day-old jelly roll
and the photo of her late husband Louis,
past the wheezing red chest
of the vintage Coke cooler
with its open door and parallel pews
of Schmidts, Storz, Buckhorn and Blatz
hanging in their steel collars,
past the jam-packed horseshoe
of the aquamarine spectators' bench
and pretty, petite, blonde-tinted Verlena Buck
at the scorer's table reading
the possibility of a perfect game,
past the impossible split
in the trousers of six-foot eight-inch,
four-hundred-pound veteran
of the Korean Police Action,
LeeRoy "The King" Buck,
past his quick *Whipdee, by Got!*
and past his life-long ignorance
of the brogue in his speech,
past the custom-made, spinless
no-English-won-hundwed-doo-send-American
two-finger bowling ball just now touching down
like an overloaded Air Force transport
two-thirds the way down the alley,
past the pins still quivering
from the last set-up,
past the greasy pin-setting machine,

past the slight gap in the fingers
and past the left eye of seventh-grade pin-girl
and third cousin to the "The King"
Teeky Bittle in a full lotus on the crash wall
peeking through,
past the discarded screwdriver, chisel,
ballpeen hammer and crowbar,
past the ripped and gaping slot machine,
past the spread of Susan B. Anthony
dollars on the floor,
kneels sideburned fifteen-year-old
make-out artist Neal Scrim,
mouth a dead zero ringed in acne,
suspecting nothing.

Something for the Telling

In each telling the madness of it
comes on me again –
the sledgehammer pulse,
the crystalline night vision.
Even in my old age my nostrils flare
to the smell of tequila at the thought,
my throat thickens in each telling,
and the piebald hand
resting on my stick steadies again.

A Sunday the summer of the drought
after Earl died, meant for drinking a curse
on the heat, the dry grass,
the fireweed sprouting up in the hay meadows,
on skinny cows going dry on their calves,
a curse on dervish windmills
pumping as much sand as water,
on the wind
and on Earl for leaving the place to me.
That summer we woke to the wind,
worked with wind at our elbows,
in our ears,
the sand it carried in our teeth,
under our skins,
until at night it entered our dreams
as the voices of the ghosts of the Sioux
saying our sins against the spirit of the wind.
That's the way it was that afternoon,
drinking and picking the blistered skin
beneath our mustaches,
cursing and scared we'd been cursed,

when Jackson thought to drink a curse
on Wesley and his no-good brother Billy
who lived four miles south

down on the county line,
who that spring had put in center-pivot irrigation
to suck up everybody's water
at a thousand gallons a minute.
The more we thought about it
and those dead Indians,
the more we listened to the wind,
the surer we were
it was Wesley and his worthless brother,
and just as the sun set
Jackson remembered the dynamite.

Earl had had it around for years,
and Jackson had seen him handle it
once to blow up a stump,
and he figured he'd seen enough
to make it work again.
We found it by match-light in the shed.
The horses must have smelled our breath
or read our minds and gave us some trouble,
so, balancing on top the corral gate,
I told them that what we were about to do
had religious significance, was big medicine,
while Jackson walked between them
and got a tight hand on their near ears.
We saddled up as clouds moved
on the rising moon, blotting out the stars,
and rode off with our shirts and saddlebags
stuffed with sticks, caps, tape, fuse and a bottle.

The gods that govern madness gave us
sure hands that night as we worked our way
from tower to tower
toward the center of the field,
placing the caps
where they seemed to want to go,
taping bundles together,

taping each bundle
where it looked like it'd do some damage,
stringing the long fuse,
while first a veil covered the moon,
then a haze,
then a fog,
on skittish horses
all bunched up beneath us,
ready to fly at the littlest change in the wind.
We were just taping the last bundle on the pump
when we saw how the gods had tricked us:
We sat our horses in the middle of the field;
the lighting end of the fuse was in our hands.
We ciphered two ways out:
across rows of tall corn
or racing fire back down the lane we'd come up,
a quarter-mile fuse running
through eleven bundles of ten sticks each.
Sheet lightning danced in the west.
We listened to the wind for guidance.
I was just sobering up
enough to know better
when I heard nothing:
For the first time that summer
the wind had paused.
The match blazed
and burned in stillness.
Jackson touched off the fuse
and we spurred our horses.

Oh, we were maybe fifty yards
ahead of the first explosion,
so bright and loud
it was like riding lightning
through the middle of summer thunder.
The concussion set off a thousand gallons
of diesel in the tank by the pump

and lifted the horses into the air.
We came down on all four
a few feet farther down the lane,
and we didn't need spurs again.
I saw the flash of the second bang
reflected in a horse's eye.
I turned to look just once,
and it was like someone had dropped
a kid's erector set into a coal furnace.
Someplace in that ride Jackson lost his hat,
I lost most of the hearing in one ear,
and the horses' tails got singed pretty good.
Just shy of the road we were blown away
from the gate into the corn,
and we jumped four strands of barbed wire
on the wind from the last bundle.

Even now I'm sitting a blowing horse
on a rise a mile away,
watching a diesel fire puddle
and spread among flattened pipe,
bent galvanized and green corn.
Even now I see the squat column
of water stand in the fire,
and even now the wind brings Earl's laugh
across decades into my deaf ear.

Weather in the Bones

An old man's bones know two things:
The dance changing weather makes
along the welds of ribs cracked
and fingers snapped in his youth,
each hairline fracture or clean break
stepping to the tune of changing
temperature, pressure and humidity;
and the past, all of it locked in calcium
surer than the brain can hold it
in its fading little electrical storm.
Sometimes it's as if I am a young man
standing on a hill in wet grass
watching that storm recede,
its distant lightning a glowing pulse,
thunder less than an echo.
It's then I feel the cold and balmy
weathers that were my life
and listen to what my bones recall.

We gathered LeeRoy and Verlena's cattle
all of two days and a morning,
skinny cows,
each hide a sack hung over a frame of bones,
and stunted calves
stupid in starvation and heat.
The wind that blew all summer
like fire over the prairie
paused as if to savor the sale,
relaxing a moment during a job well started.
We dredged the pastures,
animals fetlock-deep in sand,
feathers of dust rising from every hoof,
brought them together at the rodeo grounds,

made the best sort we could

and sat our horses waiting.
We chewed leaf tobacco
to keep the spit in our mouths
and passed a bottle
to keep from saying again
what saying couldn't help.
We faced southwest,
where summer storms once had come,
but only the haze of kicked-up dust
colored the skyline there.
Even Jackson's big buckskin
Karl hung his head at loose reins' end.

They started coming by the family first,
none with the cash or the grass to take the cattle,
as if in rehearsal
for what was sure to come in time for them.
Wind-burnt men spat little puddles
in the dust between their feet,
heads drooping like played-out horses.
Women stared into the sun,
eyes shaded by raw hands
held parallel to a burned land,
looking after children in clothes
frayed and bleached as oat stubble.
The auctioneer showed.
In the voice an undertaker uses to the grieved,
he told us how it would be,
and LeeRoy,
whose consonants had always been twisted and tied,
gave his short answers soft and clear.
Calves cried weak as sheep to the cows' hoarse bellers.
Buyers from Cheyenne and Denver descended like buzzards.

I thought it was the auctioneer's amplified voice
that made Karl throw his head up and ears forward
until I saw the dust funneling

in and out of his flared nostrils.
And LeeRoy was sucking air, too,
as if his body were a child's balloon
he was blowing up to his giant proportions.
Still, to the southwest lay only a ragged quilt
of yellow prairie and blue-white sky.
The cattle began to mill in the corrals,
then something ran through the crowd
like a wind beneath the auctioneer's spiel.
My mare wanted to curl around
and faunched her weight from leg to leg.
That was when the first gust
climbed the buttons of my spine
like chilled fingers running a keyboard.
I gave the mare her head,
and through the grit in my eyes saw blue
thunderheads piling high to the north.

The sun burned our eyes,
and we tasted sand on the wind.
The storm held its distance, built and rolled higher.
The auctioneer stammered, started again and stopped.
LeeRoy jumped up on the block,
knocked the auctioneer away with one hand
and plucked the microphone with the other.
I smell it, he said. *Dere ain't gohna be no sale!*
Verlena stood at the end of her rein
staring across at the roiling clouds,
body braced as if against a board.
We heard the first thunder.
The storm towered higher in the heavens.
The sun was gone
as if someone had passed a hand over it,

and still the rain held back.
Jackson found a shotgun and fired into the sky.
The first drops hit so slow I could count them,

each kicking up dust, settling into its little crater.
The rhythm quickened,
and rain hammered my upturned face.
My tongue swelled with it,
and my lips moved as if to nurse.
Verlena stood beneath a sopping hatbrim.
Her shoulders slackened
as if she'd let down some great weight,
and her knees began to buckle.
Over the boom of thunder
and the crackle of the PA shorting out
I heard a shout and turned to see
LeeRoy lift his bulk from a standing start,
fly through wet air
and land both feet square beside her.
His thumbs and fingertips met around her waist.
He lifted her high toward the lowering clouds
and circled and circled,
toe-behind-heel-turn,
toe-behind-heel-turn,
orbiting her suspended form,
eyes to eyes across three feet of storm,
until she found his head in her arms.
Joined in that embrace they were one
figure in the sweeping sheets of rain.

Oh, my bones recollect more of that time,
the crack and splinter of corral boards
when spooked cattle broke for open land,
the crush of beef that sent my mare down,
the horn that hooked me
and the hoof that snapped my wrist,
but the ache and throb there when rain nears
is a bright memory of black clouds, mud
and two people who waltzed in that weather.

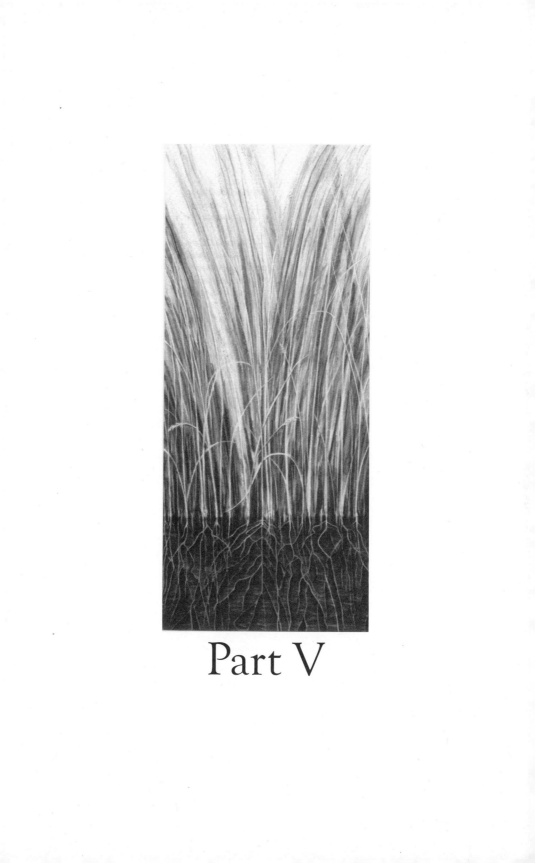

Part V

Shipped to the Americas

– "The first half of life is spent saying hello . . ."

Every good choice no less than bad
    sets up hard as a brick until choices
stack up yards high into hard walls of blessings –
family, friends, what the community calls position –
mortared by habit and ambition till we seem
only inmates taking our exercise
in this narrow space of our own making.

Saints among sinners, we uniformly shamble
to the cadence of a smoker's cough
on knees blown out in sport.
On visitors' day, the young wonder
at the distance imposed between us,
can't understand why Daddy's locked up in this place.
Daddy's doing time, though nobody knows his crime.

Preacher's hunkered down along the wall,
getting some winter sun on his pale face,
working the kinks out of his stiffened hands
with the rest of us. He says, *Lookie here,*
this ain't right! I'm an innocent man.
I didn't do nothing to deserve this! Old-timers
look away, smiles playing their lips like banjos.

It comes with the territory, Salesman says.
I made a good living. I got three daughters
on the outside I raised proper.
I paid my taxes, didn't cheat on my wife.
We're bored, already wondering what's on TV.
The sun sets pale behind the wall. He considers.
This ain't bad, like what time done to Mom and Pop.

Rats running all hours

JV Brummels

beneath the roof.
No novocaine nor ether,
and a black rotten tooth.
The folks just two old fools
waiting it out, seeing it through.

Cold, we button collar buttons on our faded blues
with swelling fingers, pull our numbered denim jackets
tight around our shoulders. Our frosted breath balloons.
Our words might just as well be icicles,
Counterfeiter opines. *It's the way people*
at all those straight jobs I kept for cover often
acted cordial but were never truly pleasant.

Night sky narrows above, cut by walls we built
to a grave shape. *Hell, we're the lucky ones,*
Gambler says. *Our numbers could've been up years ago.*
Look at the run we've had. Sure, the odds are long
against us now, but maybe there's still a chance.
We drag our arms across runny noses.
Freezing snot on worn sleeves refracts the starlight.

Bright star, get me away from this cold ground,
get me a fast car to some hot-sun town.
Find me a stack of cash and my chrome-plate forty-five,
a traveling redhead who don't know the math.
Lord, fly my righteous ass out of here
and set it down by a river of cold beer.

Flat Earthers

Twenty-five-hundred years
   after Pythagoras took the measure
of the hypotenuse, a genetically engineered,
square-hipped Holstein in Wayne County
lets slip the milkers, mounts the ramp
out a rectangle of door, threads a cramped alley
past the standing stalls of a thousand of her sisters,
all while beneath her cloven hoofs
the ball of earth turns itself daily
and above the roof the round sun burns
hurling along an arcing trajectory
among an incalculable round number
of silent, disapproving stars.

Bones

The backhoe man wears black. I suppose
the dirt and grease of his work don't show
that way. Today, he plays undertaker

to the first horse I ever bought.
For this man it's a pretty good fit.
He sympathizes. I wouldn't pay

for a hole for just any horse, but this mare
carried my kids when they were little,
and the cowboys I know knew her well.

They'll want to pay their respects. *I just*
don't want the dogs dragging her
piece by piece up to the house, I say.

What I don't tell him is she died pawing
the ground and staring off to the south,
in the distance something only she could see.

*   *   *

Still, by the next spring, the coyotes
have made a den of the grave's soft earth,
and they've drug these few dark long bones

out to bleach in the sun. The truth is,
I don't much mind. If we know anything
it's that flesh feeds the living.

Death instructs us. These bones
are rock in their heft, a weight
beyond cow or dog or bird,

a dense history of evolution

from some soft-soled, multi-toed swamp-dweller
to leg and hoof that hammer down distance.

I gather these, one by one, into the cradle
of my arms, carry back to the hole what carried me
so many miles, lay them back away

and stand bareheaded before this grave.
Death questions us. New grass
is the soft, shining hide draped

on the flesh of earth, and rock her bones.
Or this hole is just another hungry mouth
and earth the final carnivore who feeds

on flesh that's only meat, gnaws bones to dust.
I stomp dirt down to keep the light at bay,
mount the impatient horse that today

carries my flesh through these hills
and ride away.

   —for Paul Zarzyski and Lizzie D.

Coyote Vision

Some people fear the shadow world,
but some people aren't coyotes
who know shadows to be true and best.

They're yipping away when I step out back,
tired of the yap of television,
cramped by two days in the city,
stiff from a night in a bad bed
and grieving for my friend two weeks dead.

I choose to walk to check the weather.
Our big dog steps down the lane with me,
twice barks his hollow scared-of-the-shadows bark.
The coyotes' yelps fade into the night.
I'm headed south up the abandoned road
to see what I can from the top of my world.

The moon's on the skyline,
my dead friend's moon,
a blue fruit cupped in yellow horns
the night we got the phone call,
but tonight, three days past full,
bright enough that when I check my heel
I mistake the shadow dog for the real.

I name the horses in their trap
by shape and shade as I pass.
The farthest from the fence,
on a little roll of earth,
lifts his head, ears pitched, when I call.
Horse or shadow of horse, I'm not sure at all.

*

And when I pass my boundary fence
I fall headlong into a bramble of shadow.

Moonlight through the thicket
of chokecherry atop of the cutbank
scratches in the pale dust of the trail
like an illustration from some grim tale
of deep, dangerous woods
and some child stranded
there on a living journey
with goblins everywhere.

On my face a warning breeze.
The big dog's gone.
The coyotes keep their peace.

In a strobe of nerves
I know it's my friend
I'm climbing this hill to see,
away from condolences and family and TV.
These branching shadows I stand among
are ganglia, a deep reach
past moonlit flesh to where maybe
the recognizable spirit lives still.
Our certain and terrible deaths
is the truth we hide
among the clutter
of our brightly lit and civilized lives.

Still, I have had faith in the wisdom
of many forms without substance –
dead, he is no less friend.
I drag ahead a heavy boot
on a leg like lead.
All I can know waits
within this thicket of shadow.

*

I stand in weather atop my world.
The moon showers me with generous light.

JV Brummels

In the distance the city my friend left behind
sends its industrial glare into the sky.
Among the dark shapes of roadside brush
a coyote's hind leg flashes in a flush
of yellow light. The fine ruff
of hair on my neck bristles in recognition.

When I turn, the path home is clear,
the moon riding high in the sky.
The big dog sniffs out mice in the grass,
pounces and misses, by a mile, the mark,
like anyone domestic supposing in the dark.

Cry Like a Girl

"Black for them is evil or random or unknown. Black robs
the mind of sight. It is the collapse of the whole universe."
—Walter Mosley

After nights of a waxing moon on snow
I'm caught outside in an inky cloud
so dense I can't make out the yellow shed,
jump as if shocked when my stretched fingers
contact its steel side. A night so black
I look back to the window-lit house
to check if I've been struck blind,
the animal spark that brings me out
to prowl each night for once arrested.

The curtained light of my daughter's room
belies the inky funk she's fallen into
this near her seventeenth birthday.
I bought this wool shirt last winter
in an unpredicted cold snap
on a three-day visit to a city hospital
to rebuild her auto-wrecked knee.
She liked the morphine,
swam out of it long enough to explain
my lame joke to her mother
while on the TV some other man's daughter
married a millionaire she'd never met.

The light blinks out, leaving me
lost in the dark on ground I own,
fool to the fiction
that to have and to know are one.
Warm shirt or no, I won't last till sunup,
but I don't have the sense to negotiate
the ice and tangle of firewood
between me and the house. Besides,

I'm lost in the cave of my mind
among an old man's book,
the mellow call of a tenor sax,
the cost of a hard day's work
toddling after the one before,
and a lens of tears can't brighten that dark.

I wait for some thrum of vision
to get me past all my spirit's scattered trash.
What I know is fantasy.
I'm a rogue electron in erratic orbit,
more contrary than independent,
blind to cycles of tide and moon.
Lone male in a house of women,
I've latched on to my daughter's PMS and cramps.
Maybe it's hormones that make us human.
As my daughter's father, I never knew
what to do, only that my guesses had to be true.
At the end of her first hospital stay,
when she was six and we thought
we'd lost her, I found her early the day
she was to go home, sitting in the room alone
in a chair staring over a different city's skyline,
reflected in her dry eyes a world of coming light.

Back when emigrants boarded ships
as if embarking for the stars, I saw
in black and white the news of a family fleeing
a British bust for an Australian boom.
The camera stayed long on an old man's eyes,
him on the dock saying goodbye
to children and grandchildren he'd never see
again. I wept then to see those old eyes,
but only now I know what he had to do
after the camera crew packed up their gear
and drove off, and the ship steamed away
and away till he couldn't see it anymore –

he had to wipe his eyes, turn
and make his way to his own back door.

The Wide Poem

"The moral high ground's the most expensive real estate in the world."

A fullblood I met told me Lakota has no word
for wilderness. Teachers taught me Puritans –
my forefathers – coupled wilderness and evil.
Some claim this is the last holy land. Here,
at ninety-four hundred feet, the Department
of Interior sign makes it official Wilderness.
What do we know for sure? Every square foot
of earth is numbered by global positioning satellites.

I'll select my own pedigree, and pilgrims
have nothing to do with me, except I fit my feet
with care between rocks in tracks of those
who've made this trek before. What to think,
when long shadows from high rocks so ancient
they may be all we ever know of eternity
crawl through the thin air to us? That the wild
geography we long to learn always lies just within.

Thursday Night Special

I can tell you what hasn't happened yet,
an unearned vision of a January Saturday
in the rain astride a borrowed horse
trailing black cattle across Antelope County
off the divide into the valley of the Elkhorn
down to just shy of the old Black Hills Road,
some place west of the North Fork,
some time that side of tomorrow.

*

But the past is all that's guaranteed,
the weather forecast full of holes
as my deck of missing cards.
Friday we loaded Buck and Joe
in weather soft and white as milktoast,
trailered down to the county line,
gathered the second-calvers
and, dressed thin in the dropping sun,
drove them into the heart of an evil cold fog.
We penned the cattle,
tethered the horses by their reins
and stood in our mud-caked boots
on Elaine's entryway rug
sucking down hot coffee.
I knew then that spot was as near
the river as I'd get that weekend,
six miles uphill in the fog
cozier than sixty upstream.

*

But even the past can fade in and out,
like my visible breath in this surefire present,
a warm Tuesday evening in April,

91

the second-calvers trucked home a month ago
and with the herd tending this season's young
under the stars in the red-grass hills
out behind the barn I've got my back to,
that breath rising to join clouds
I predict will bring the next spring rain
to someone someplace sometime.

        *

If earth be round and seasons cycle
I can on this cusp
recall a future and predict a past.
I flick the tipend of my smoke
to the packed mud between the barns,
a token of the grass that grew there
before ever we were conceived,
a sign of what will come to be
after these barns are gone,
foundations scoured to dust
by the breath of wind that survives us,
of the grass that will cover us,
of the grass we will become.

Book of Grass is JV Brummels' fourth collection of poetry. He has published a novel and short fiction, edited several anthologies and the literary magazine *Nebraska Territory*, and serves as the publisher of Logan House. A long-time member of the faculty of Wayne State College, he lives on a ranch in northern Nebraska.